I put pen to paper
writing my words on water,
brush to canvas
smudging my colors onto the wind;
and all the while
knowing the impermanence
of it all.

~ *Candice James*

(excerpt from "Ink and Colors" pg. 32)

Also by Candice James

Blue Silence *(Silver Bow Publishing) 2024*
Short Shots 2 *(Silver Bow Publishing) 2023*
Spiritual Whispers *(Silver Bow Publishing) 2023*
Imagination's Reverie *(Silver Bow Publishing) 2023*
Atmospheres *(Silver Bow Publishing) 2023*
The Depth of the Dance *(Silver Bow Publishing)* 2023
Behind the One-Way Mirror *(Silver Bow Publishing)* 2022
The Call of the Crow *(Silver Bow Publishing)* 2021
The Path of Loneliness *(Inanna Publications)* 2020
Rithimus Aeternam *(Silver Bow Publishing)* 2019
Haiku Paintings *(Silver Bow Publishing)* 2019
The 13th Cusp *(Silver Bow Publishing)* 2018
Fhaze-ing *(Silver Bow Publishing)* 2018
The Water Poems *(Ekstasis Editions)* 2017
Short Shots *(Silver Bow Publishing)* 2016
City of Dreams *(Silver Bow Publishing)* 2016
Merging Dimensions *(Ekstasis Editions)* 2015
Colors of India *(Xpress Publications India)* 2015
Purple Haze *(Libros Libertad)* 2014
A Silence of Echoes *(Silver Bow Publishing)* 2014
Shorelines *(Silver Bow Publishing)* 2013
Ekphrasticism *(Silver Bow Publishing)* 2013
Midnight Embers *(Libros Libertad)* 2012
Bridges and Clouds *(Silver Bow Publishing)* 2011
Inner Heart, a Journey *(Silver Bow Publishing)* 2010
A Split in the Water *(Fiddlehead Poetry Books)* 1979

the still
small voice
of soul

by

Candice James

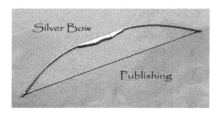

Box 5 – 720 – 6th Street,
New Westminster, BC
V3C 3C5   CANADA

Title: the still small voice of soul
Author: Candice James
Cover Painting: *"Bay of Fundy Sundown,*
                New Brunswick, Canada"
                painting by Candice James
Layout/Design: Candice James
ISBN: 978177403-320-3(print)
ISBN: 978177403 319-7(ebk)j

© Silver Bow Publishing 2024

Library and Archives Canada Cataloguing in Publication

Title: The still small voice of soul / Candice James.
Names: James, Candice, 1948- author.
Identifiers: Canadiana (print) 20240475534 |
Canadiana (ebook) 20240475542 | ISBN
9781774033203
   (softcover) | ISBN 9781774033197 (Kindle)
Subjects: LCGFT: Poetry.
Classification: LCC PS8569.A429 S75 2024 | DDC
C811/.54—dc23

And the waves …
oh the beautiful sparkling waves
of the whispering cosmic sea.

And the waters …
oh the calming, soothing waters
of heaven's sea.

~ Candice James

(excerpt from "Sanctified Shores" pg. 39)

the still small voice of soul -Candice James

CONTENTS

A Silence Deeper / 11
A Very Brief Moment / 12
All Time Is Happening Now / 13
As You Live In Me / 14
At The Quantum Level / 15
Becoming/Looking / 16
Begat / 17
Blowing Kisses To The Wind / 18
Burnt-Out Stars / 19
Childhood Is Gone /20
Nicomekl River / 21
Dead To Me / 22
Far From Yesterday's Light / 23
Fingerprints / 24
Flightless / 25
Forever Young And Beautiful / 26
Ghostly Feel / 27
Guilty / 28
I Am Here / 29
I Am The Magician / 30
I Close My Eyes / 31
Ink And Colors / 32
Interrogatory Man / 33
Into The Impending Sweet / 34
Moments When / 35
Mystical Moment / 36

Predestined / 37
Quiet Angel / 38
Sanctified Shores / 39
Scissors / 40
Softly Lit Hallway /41
Sometimes When I Lay Down / 42
Still I Think On You / 43
Sweet Dreams Of You / 44
Tangible Dream / 45
Teacher/Student / 46
The Drowning / 47
The Signature / 48
The Veil / 49
The Weeping Willows / 50
Thinking Of You / 51
Two Sides Of The Reversible Coat / 52
Under A Sky Of Sheen / 53
Up And Down Ladders / 54
The Wisdom Of Karma / 55
Wading The Shallows / 56
We Are Made For Pain / 57
When The Snow Falls / 58
Whisper / 59
Who I Am / 60
Wishing Stones / 61
Wrapped, Cloaked And Shawled / 62
Yet Again / 63
A Heart Full / 64

White, Silvery Dream / 65
Always I Am With You / 66
As I Awaken / 67
Beach / 68
But You Are / 69
Crimson Watering Can / 70
Pale Grey Tombstone / 71
Familiar Angels / 72
Fire And Frost / 73
Dear Dead People / 74
Casting Off / 75
And The Book Closes / 76

the still small voice of soul -Candice James

A Silence Deeper

All day I've watched the snowflakes fall
whispering secrets to the sky;
and though I try in vain to hear them,
silently they melt and disappear
and I am left to wonder at the wonder
of the God who built this beautiful world
as winter's whiteness is unfurled.

There is a silence to this white world.
A silence deeper than the deepest quiet.

All day I've watched the snowflakes fall.
Night is falling and it's lost its dark cloak.
The white snow blankets the ground
and wraps around the trees
creating a quasi-daylight scene.

Oh night ... where is your dark?
It has succumbed to Nature's white knife.
It has been murdered unceremoniously
and I for one am glad as I look outside
onto this winter wonderland.

There is a silence to this white world.
A silence deeper than the deepest quiet.

A Very Brief Moment

I saw roses blooming
on a dune of crystal snow;
and I saw violets springing
on a burning desert dune.

I traveled further from my rest

      and then...

I saw sandcastles
suspended in the air;
and I saw tulips
growing in the sand.

And for a moment,
a very brief moment,
I thought you could be mine,

All Time Is Happening Now

There's a photo of me as a toddler
that sits on my night table.

I think of my mother standing
just out of sight in that photo;
and I think on how she meant
only the best for me in everything she did.

And today, I think of how I always
went against what she told me
and it keeps running through my mind
as I look at the picture and say,
"Listen to your mother Candice;
listen to your mother."

I say it hoping to influence my past.

Scientists say all time is happening now.
So, I believe, somehow,
I have influenced my past
and that is the main reason
I am who I am today.

It could have all turned out so differently.
I could have died long ago on that other path
I was traveling down.

As You Live In Me

I scratch words and symbols
onto the northeast wind
to send love letters
straight to your soul;
and if perchance
the arrows they ride on
pierce your heart
and scratch my initials into it
then a part of me
will live in you forever —
as you live in me
everyday of my life.

At The Quantum Level

The world passes by
in colors, scents, and music:
        Sometimes a lullaby.
        Sometimes an opera.

As these things pass by,
they pass through you.

Some leave a part of themselves
       with you.

Some are just visitors.

      BUT
   all impact you
at the quantum level.

Becoming/Looking

It's like a gull gliding high in the sky
turning into a snow-white dove.
Like a rowboat on the ocean
turning into a sailboat
when the sun is ablaze
and the warm winds gently blow.

It's like me becoming
a vision of love
whenever I look at you.

It's like a caterpillar on a branch
turning into a butterfly.
Like a tulip in the garden
turning into a red, red rose
when the rain is silk
and the grass a dampened sheet.

It's like me becoming
a sweet, sweet dream
whenever you look at me.

Begat

On the shores of my soul
waves of discontent and dissonance
lap at my sullen silence
      begat from a wound
      too deep to speak of;
      begat from the name
      I whisper in my sleep.

On the shores of my heart
your ghost treads softly
through my night
and speaks to my soul
in whispers and sighs.

      Heart and soul
      you are with me
         always ...
         always.

Begat from the ache in my being.

Blowing Kisses To The Wind

Dark figures stroll the canyons of my mind
whispering in raspy voices,
throwing open locked doors,
rummaging through unspeakable secrets.

But the secrets have voices of their own
and they won't stay silenced.
I cover the ears of my soul
and try to find solace in an old dream
that has no threatening edges.

I lift my eyelids and gaze outside.
At the end of the driveway
I see your familiar ghost
blowing kisses to the wind
but never to me ... never to me.

Always it's you at the edge of the firs.
Always just out of reach of my heart
and forever lost to my soul.

Burnt Out Stars

I laid my dreams on the quilt
of a yesterday memory
and wished on a long ago
burnt out star.

I knew when I made the wish
it wouldn't come true,
but still a part of me
believed it might come true.

This is the way of a dreamer
who doesn't live in the real world.
This is the way of a lost Bo-Peep
who keeps hoping, against hope,
the lambs will find her
and show her the way to go home.

If wishes were lambs
she might find her way home.
If burnt out stars could shine
I might find my way to your heart.

But this world is not made for dreamers.
And sadly, I've finally come to realize,
burnt out stars can never shine;
and you were not meant to be mine.

Childhood Is Gone

There's a crepe paper feel
to these thoughts in my mind:
Crinkly. Squishy.
Like dry leaves and damp sand.

There's a sky and a beach
where never the twain shall meet;
where I hover above,
like a hazy ghost,
surrounded by dragonflies
and birdsong.

It's a magical merry-go-round
      kind of day
in the amusement park
      of my mind.

            Come back Peter.
            Come back Paul.

But they no longer answer
      to my call.
They're dancing now
to someone else's song
   and alas, alack ...
 childhood is gone.

Nicomekl River

At the edge of the Nikomekl River,
near where it flows into the ocean
a little south of the Crescent Beach pier,
I skipped stones on an early August morning
and sang an unwritten love song to you.

The warm west wind rushed in like a lion.
The autumn leaves turned to snow
and the years flew by like runaway kites.

Some distant tomorrow I'll stand
at the edge of the Nikomekl River
and skip stones again as I recall
another day long ago
when I sang an unwritten love song to you
before you drifted far away from me.

And I'll sigh and wonder where you are.

Dead To Me

In the best part of my mind
parts of you are slipping away
in a gradual movement of cleansing.

One day I won't remember who you are,
or what you meant to me,
or even why I cared.

In my eyes you will only be
the reflection of a stranger
who once touched my heart.

You will slowly cease to exist
in my little world of worlds.

Your eyes will no longer seem familiar
and you will no longer be in me,
in my thoughts, in my heart.

You will be dead to me
almost like you never were.

Far From Yesterday's Light

The ancient days of me and you
are blurred inside the fading blue.

Those days are gone that meant the most;
and now, to you, I'm just a ghost.

Oh, sad world of relentless pain,
shall I never hold you close again?

In this life we pass each other
hazy ghosts in the night,
estranged in a strange land,
far from yesterday's light.

Fingerprints

Love leaves its fingerprints
embedded in the heart
and aglow in the mind —
embers of memories still burning
ready to burst into flame
at the heart's beckoning;
at the very thought of you.

You do not belong to me
on so many levels
but you do belong to me
on one level.

The level of luminescent spirit,
witnessed by the lingering remnants
of your misty breath
on the mirror of my soul.

Flightless

With crows on my shoulders
I should be able to free my spirit
and fly high and away with you.

But I can't.

No matter how I try
I can't fly to you
because your heart is closed.

So I will loose these crows forever
and continue walking through my world
        flightless
                ... without you.

Forever Young And Beautiful

On the dark side of the mountain
              called night
I lie on a blanket of sleeping dreams
and each breath brings me closer to you

In this place of long swaying shadows
I stumble into the arms of yesterday
and I see you in a painting being painted
by my ghost that lives in another dimension.

I am the surgeon of the palette knife.
I am the seamstress of the brush.
I am the mix and tincture of the color.
You are the masterpiece I have created
in my memory, my mind and my being.

After the paint has dried
and the canvas is quiet
this moment of indelible moments isn't new...
I recognize it from the many dreams
I dreamed of you
in the many lifetimes I've lived.
Yesterday, today, tomorrow and forever
your image in my eyes never changes.
You are always forever young and beautiful
to me and you'll always be.

Ghostly Feel

A light January rain
drizzles onto the vehicles
on the rooftop parking lot.
    A seagull careens in
        and alights
on a silver air vent pipe.

The sky is a nondescript pale gray
and the horizon a blur
of fog and mist.

There is an otherworldly,
ghostly feel to this day.
        Damp,
      nondescript
      and blurry.

A surreal watercolor painting
viewed through veiled eyes
    and a weary heart.

Guilty

Ransacked nights
of stardust and teardrops,
still hold the ragged remnants
of the lovers we used to be.

There's an old bus stop bench,
with our invisible initials carved in it,
that still sits at the corner
of Braid and Columbia street
in another dimension
just beyond my reach.

And ... there's a phantom bus
with a ghostly driver
waiting to pick me up again
at the crossroads
of love and lust,
where grace and sin hold hands
and I am found guilty
of loving you — once again.

I Am Here

Your face takes on a glow
when you smile;
then I'm lost in the promise
I see in your eyes.

Somewhere there is a cat
abandoned on a dark street.
Somewhere there is a dog
alone and longing for warmth.

Somewhere there is a hungry heart
alone and longing for love.

And I am here,
wrapped in my loneliness,
longing for your touch.

I Am The Magician

I pleat the clouds in my eyes
and paint a dissolving illusion.

I am the magician
of the disappearing dream.

If you blow on my cheek,
I'll kiss the rabbit
back into the hat.

I am the one you've been waiting for.

I have arrived,
I am the magician.

Take my hand
and I'll tell you all my secrets
and loose the doves
in our hearts.

I Close My Eyes

I close my eyes
and concentrate
to send you visions
soft and alluring.

I imagine you
are closing in on me.
and I draw a sweeter breath.

I close my eyes
and concentrate.
trying to close in on you
wherever you are.

Always ...
you're my desire.

Ink And Colors

In this oblique universe
we are suspended between
an elliptical sky above
and a circular world below.

Infinite emptiness above.
Crumbling solidity below.

Ink and colours:

I put pen to paper
writing my words on water,
brush to canvas
smudging my colors onto the wind;
and all the while
knowing the impermanence of it all.

Interrogatory Man

You are
an unanswerable question,
an unscalable mountain
and an unsailable sea.

But deep in the far reaches
of your unconquerable heart
I see pieces of your shining soul
and I hear it screaming to be saved.

I will
climb your mountain
and sail your sea.
I will find the answer to you
and you will be my answer
and no longer a question
in a world of confused chaos.

Interrogatory man ...
you are my Rubik's cube.

Into The Impending Sweet

My voice bounces back to me
in shades of luminous blue
and I am lost in a melody
that reminds me of you.

Echoes of yesterday voices
invade the dark of my light
and cut the edge of my bright
enfolding me into the night.

And there,
at that darkened edge of day,
I climb into the impending sweet
where I can lose myself in dreams ...
sweet, sweet dreams of you.

Moments When

There are moments when I see you
and I seem to know you well.
Then there are moments
when I look at you and realize
I don't know you at all.
But something deep in me
says I know you well
even though all things
would seem to say I don't.

Time, space, the world,
people, hearts, souls
all passing by in a whirl
and it seems to me
we've sat like this before
and laughed like this before
somewhere in time
long ago and far away
but I can't quite remember
the time or the place.

Yes ... there are moments;
    moments when
I think I know you well.

Mystical Moment

In the gleaning of a mystical moment
and the opening of long-ago doors,
I saw us as we used to be.
When you were mine
and I was yours.

We stood on high ground
above a glittering city
of sights and sounds
and memories;
dreams driving cars
weaving through the stars
and we were oblivious to all
except ourselves
in that long ago mystical moment
I wish could come again.

Predestined

I hear another plane passing overhead
　　　and I wonder,
if just one person's number is up
　　　on that plane,
are the rest of the passengers
forced to depart this realm early?

Do chance and luck
play an integral part
in life and death?
　　　Or,
is it all predestined.

Quiet Angel

The midnight ocean is calling to me,
calling me out to the sea.
To the sea of forgetfulness,
forgotten dreams and lost wishes
where I dance with you
to tender love songs.

There's a quiet angel
waiting for me.
Waiting to take me back home.

Soon an ocean of sky
and beautiful music
will call to me
and a quiet angel
will whisper my name
and I'll dance with you once again.

Sanctified Shores

Agate, coral, topaz and rose quartz
decorate the beaches in my mind.

And the waves ...
oh the beautiful sparkling waves
of the whispering cosmic sea.

And the waters ...
oh the calming, soothing waters
of heaven's sea.

The waves and the waters
rejuvenate my weary sinking soul
and lift if to drift and wash
onto sanctified shores
that it may fall asleep
on the glittering beach
of a long-ago dream
that's coming true at last.

Scissors

I have fashioned silky scissors
to gently cut my way into your heart
so I will know who you really are
and you will know who I really am.

As long as there are lovers
there will be scissors to cut.
Some, silky with gentle incursions.
Some, steely with harsh thrusts.

As long as there are scissors
there will be lovers to use them
to gently part the emotions
or harshly wound the soul.

And even though you'll never be mine
I'll fall asleep to dream of you
and cut my way into your dreams
with these silky scissors
I've fashioned for only you.

Softly Lit Hallway

Edging through a softly lit hallway
I search for the door to you
knowing, even if I find it,
I don't have the key.

I've long since tried all the windows,
never being able to open them;
only able to peek through the slats
of your slightly closed venetian blinds.

You are an enigma;
an unsolvable puzzle
with a missing piece.

Edging through the softly lit hallway,
I see the exit sign and realize
there's no way into you
        for me.

Sometimes When I Lay Down

Sometimes, almost asleep in the dark,
I can feel something otherworldly nearby.
A shadow within the shadow of a shadow
that knows my name; hears my heartbeat.
There is a fear coupled with a welcoming
that fills my being to overflowing,
      And I think:
Is this the spirit of someone I know
who passed away into the realm beyond?
or is it a living person in spirit form
who has come to my side with desire.

Sometimes, almost asleep in the dark,
I'm afraid to move or even fall asleep.
Other times I am calm and assured
it's probably someone who loves me.

I believe it is you manifesting
out of the ether in spirit form
just to be near me even though
the waking world keeps us apart.

Sometimes when I lay down to sleep
      in the dark
I can feel your heart beating ...
      inside my chest.

Still I Think On You

I am a barren field where no crops grow
the chaff of love has long been shorn
of longing, sympathy and need.
But still I think on you
and still I feel the crave
to touch your heart and feel your soul
down to its very depth,

I am a strand of silver
at odds with golden years
I am an aging shiver
locked in a falling tear,

And still I think on you
and still I feel the crave
to touch your heart and feel your soul
down to its very depth.

Alas, I am a barren field
where love has long been shorn
        of longing ...
But still ... I think on you;
and still ... I feel the crave.

Sweet Dreams Of You

I face northeast
to where you lie down to rest
and I lose myself
in sweet dreams of you.

I walk through a shaft of moonlight
that leads to your door.

The moonlight dims
then falls through
the northeast horizon
as I lay lost in sweet dreams of you ...
        lost to the world
                in sweet dreams
                        of you.

Tangible Dream

I carry my bones and age-worn flesh
down a highway of coveted dreams;
and I wish and I pray I could stay
but the dreams fade and fray at the seams.

There's a distant whisper drawing nigh
in the lilac and jasmine fields of my mind.
The spark of imagination's evolving.
My bones and flesh are slowly dissolving
as the creeping quicksand of nevermore
quickens and pulls at the root of my core.

    Opening closed doors,
        settling old scores,
in the heat of an exhaled breath
as I hold the ice-cold hands of death.

Dead dragonflies read from the scroll.
Bewitching butterflies cleanse my soul.
A growing weight falls on my chest.
I shed my weary bones and flesh,
breaking the rusty chains of life,
leaving behind this world of strife
as I walk with the saviour and the lamb
at the edge of the tangible dream I am.

Teacher / Student

The old letters of my past
keep editing and rewriting themselves
into my present, where I am creating
a new alphabet for my future.

      I am the teacher
      and I am the student.

The interchange and mingling
of maps and dreams
leads me to yesterday's sandcastles
and tomorrow's skyscrapers.

The student becomes the teacher.

      Time passes.

The teacher becomes the student
and enters the afterlife realm
for further continued education
in the creation of new letters
alphabets and numbers...
and the simple art of living
      simply.

The Drowning

In the slanted shadow of trees
I walk through a forest
of lost horizons and dreams.

I see you wandering on distant cliffs
just out of my reach.
You haze in and out
of the high drifting clouds
that peek through the fog of an old memory.

And what of the waves below
crashing the shoreline
of shipwrecks and shells?
And what of the sandcastles I built
that were washed away
in the tears of the sea?

In the shallows of the waves,
sometimes I catch a glimpse of yesterday
when we were young ...
     before the drowning came.

The Signature

In the deep dark mirror of night
I travel the waters of timeless time
skipping and jumping through a rhyme
lost in the treble clef of your soul.
searching for the music I am.

A far away rhythm keeps beckoning me
to follow its signature to your heart.

But the farther I travel
the hazier the signature;
and I don't' think I'll ever reach
your distant, unreachable heart.

The Veil

Through the dark veil of night
I see your eyes and smile
and feel you near
in, this, my illusion of choice.

Sometime the veil is so thin
I can almost feel your breath on mine.

Sometimes the veil is so thick
I can barely recognize your face.

Most times the veil fades
in and out of reality;
        but always ...
always, it's love's illusion.

The Weeping Willows

The weeping Willows
are hanging so low
and I wonder if they're
      weeping, crying
         or
     sleeping, dying.

The weeping Willows
are hanging low

    and soon
   they'll be gone
like a forgotten song ...
    as will I.

Thinking Of You

Sometimes I dream of the thrill
of being on an out-of-control tilt-a -whirl,
Most times I feel that way
whenever you are near.

Sometimes, in my mind,
I visualize your eyes
and I fall through the eye
of imagination's needle
and swim in the sea
of a dream I created
for only you and me.

Sometimes I walk a tightrope
tied to the electricity of my thoughts
        always thinking of you
alive in the sparks of my desire.

Sometimes I dream, visualize and walk.

Most times I navigate this world alone
        thinking of you.

Two Sides Of The Reversible Coat

We've all lived through
our own personal tragedies.
Entering one door.
Exiting another door
when the tears have subsided
      temporarily.

This is the circle of life:
Boredom to happiness.
Sorrow to tears.
And the merry-go-round ride
spins until it doesn't.

The strong and the weak.
The rich and the poor.

Two sides of the reversible coat
riding the same carousel.
but on different horses.

You can tell them apart
by their steeds and saddles.

Under A Sky Of Sheen

Strolling
under a sky of sheen
my eyes saw through
the fabric of life
to the threads and weave
of the body I wear.

I saw
　　　a piece of bone,
　　　a tress of hair
　　　and a heart
beating through the shining fabric
　　　of my invincible soul.

Strolling
under a sky of sheen
　　　I came closer
　　　　　to myself.

Up And Down Ladders

Climbing and descending
the up and down ladders in my mind
I saw beautiful paintings
flashing in and out of reality,
adorning the walls,
and up in the surreal attic
   there was a candlelit room
   full of masterpieces;
masterpieces I had wanted to create.

   The age-old paint,
   still wet on the brush,
   refused to give birth
   to these rebellious works of art
   hiding inside my being,
   behind a padlocked door
   that has no key.

And now it's too late.
All the up and down ladders
   in my mind
are slowly crumbling to dust;
 and I am turning to rust.

The Wisdom Of Karma

Those vacant, yet smiling, hazel eyes
found their way into my mind
and refused to leave.

Sometimes in my dreams at night
I see those vacant, smiling, hazel eyes
and wonder at the wisdom of a karma
that allowed my unsuspecting eyes
to gaze into his yet again.

Wading The Shallows

I'm wading the shallows
of your dreams
searching for the key
to your heart.

I'm flitting in and out
of your thoughts
trying to set up
a point of contact
for future rendezvous.

I'm wading the shallows
searching for higher ground
and the pathway
that leads to you.

We Are Made For Pain

Sometimes I fly like a bird
on soiled wings of glory.

Sometimes I crash and burn
like a quickly snuffed out
four-alarm fire
that leaves no trace
it ever once raged.

In every life
some tears must spill
between the laughter and smiles.

The needle of happiness
must pierce the eye of joy
to bring the dream alive.

We are made for pain,
that we may treasure joy
and savour peace.

When The Snow Falls

When the snow falls
everything sounds quieter; softer.

There's a hush to the world
that calms the storms of life.

Inside this winter blanket
of plush white silence
there is no thunder or lighting;
only the quiet of the scene.

The world becomes
a citadel of tranquility
and the storms of life
    are held at bay ...
when the snow falls.

Whisper

I am an ember
waiting to spark into flame
when I think on you
and whisper your name.

I am a breath of air
waiting to become a breeze
when I look and see
you looking at me.

There are signs
in the stars and the moon.
There are words and rhymes
and a haunting tune.

Ash to ember to flame
whenever I whisper your name.

Who I Am

I don't write poems
to know who I am.
      I write poems to see
      who I'm becoming.

I don't survey the road
to see where I am.
      I survey the road
      to see where I'm going.

I don't look at you
to see who you are.
      I look at you
      to see who I am.

I write poems
and survey roads
      but I look at you
      to see who I am.

Wishing Stones

I need an amulet, a wishing stone
and blessings from the other side.

Luck seems to have run away
from possibility.

       I am not with you.

But chance is still hanging around
tempting and disrupting.

On my side of the fence ...
all is lost.

On your side of the fence ...
I'm on the outside.

Chances are my chances are
      slowly dissolving
into broken wishing stones
and irredeemable blessings.

Wrapped, Cloaked And Shawled

Wrapped in sunlight,
I ride the paling rays of day
into an encroaching twilight.

Cloaked in moonlight,
I sink into the fading glow
of a dissolving purple twilight.

Shawled in stars and dark sky,
a nightingale whispers softly
as I sink into the deep and comforting
waters of a technicolor sleep.

The time for dreams is at hand,

Yet Again

A ribbon of white
in the vast blue above
makes me want to be
falling in love with love
       again.

Makes me want to come in from the rain
into the sunshine and chance the pain
of another love affair biting the dust
and another shiny ring turning to rust.

I sit here, inside my reverie,
drifting and dreaming on a glass sea
looking my heart right in the face
and all I see is an empty space.

So, I look back at
the white ribbon above
and it makes me want to be
falling in love with love ...
       yet again.

A Heart Full

With a heart full
of sky and smiles
I approach you
as a child does its favorite toy;
its beloved possession.

But you don't belong to me
and you don't know my heart;
and you never will.

So I walk away ...
with a heart full
of clouds and tears.

White, Silvery Dream

Inside a white silvery dream
I'm turning, I'm burning,
I'm turning to gold.

At the sharpened edge
of a sapphire cliff
I'm falling, I'm shawling
into the dream.

On the other side
of the universe
I merge into my other self.

Always, I Am With You

I am dreaming in your dreams.
I am feeling all your feelings.

I am smiling through your eyes.
I am speaking through your lips
and kissing the winds of change
that they may bring you to me.

I am in all places.

Even when I am not beside you,
I am always with you.

I am dreaming in your dreams.

Let me be the silent joy
that moves through your dreams
into the core of your being.

I am in all places,
              but always ...

        always I am with you.

As I Awaken

Beneath the throb of my heart
there is a restlessness.

I will gather all my thoughts
and place them in
the unburnt bosom
of unkindled death.

A tinder box
ready to light my way home.

I travel the ebony pathway of death
and follow the sound of your voice
back to the song I am.

As I awaken and arise
from this tomb of soiled flesh
I evolve into spotless spirit.

Beach

Here,
at the beach,
  on the promenade trail,
   trees arch
  to scratch the wind's back.

In the fade of autumn
  and the fall of my days
I head to the cold hands and feet
  of a fast-traveling winter ...
   to become
  just a memory.

I leave behind
  white stories of dark days,
glowing poems of dying embers,
  dreams within a dream.

There,
  at another beach,
I'll wade the waters of eternity
  until you come to me.

But You Are

In a world
filled with sun and moon and stars,
I wander
an ocean-kissed beach of dreams
  chasing down your ghost.

I visualize your eyes
shining brightly
and I hear you whispering;
but I can't cross over
the invisible line in the sand
that separates us.

  I'm alone
in this world
filled with sun and moon and stars
    and you are not here...
        but...
            you are.

Crimson Watering Can

There stands
the crimson watering can

paint stretched
and peeling

under a blistering
July sun

beside the white
begonias

Pale Grey Tombstone

There stands
the pale grey tombstone

edges worn
and crumbling

under a damp
November sky

beside the wilted
roses

Familiar Angels

I will go to my childhood beach
where familiar angels
once hovered overhead.

The white silver sands
will crawl between my toes
and take my heart away.

I will wade the shoreline
and hold hands with my dreams.

The warm ocean waters
will cleanse my soul;
and my familiar angels
will know I was there.

Fire And Frost

Sometimes a deep fire
creeps into my bones
and rattles my flesh
for no apparent reason.

A pre-cursor
to spontaneous combustion?

Other times a deep frost
creeps into my blood
and rattles my heart
for no reason at all.

An omen
of impending death?

Fire and frost.

They throw dice for my demise;
and I am left to guess
which one is
the devil in disguise.

Dear Dead People

I think tonight
on the dear dead people
I've lost along my way
back toward the stars.

They are the stars
in my thoughts
that light up my soul
as I fall asleep
in the dark of night
dreaming of lost days
and the dear dead people
I've lost along my way.
The dear dead people
I miss so much
and love so dearly.

I think, tonight, on them.
I think on them
every day
and every night;
the dear dead people
I've lost along my way,

Casting Off

An expanding sphere of silence
spreads over my being
as the drums of life
ebb and flow
in sync with my fading breath.

The welcome feel
of a warm embrace
slowly fills my soul
as waves of peace and tranquility
pull me into the arms of death.

I cast off the weight
of worn-out flesh and bone
as I travel further from my home
to another realm
and my real home.

And The Book Closes

Tucked in at the edge of night
I write love letters to you
in a book you'll never see.

In the cold of dawn
you melt at my feet.

The ink dries on the page;
and the book you'll never read
            closes.